How Do Animals Give Us Food?

Linda Staniford

capstone

Edited by Helen Cox Cannons
Designed by Steve Mead
Original illustrations © Capstone Global Library Limited 2016
Illustrated by Steve Mead
Picture research by Tracy Cummins
Production by Victoria Fitzgerald
Originated by Capstone Global Library Limited

Library of Congress Cataloging-in-Publication Data
Names: Staniford, Linda, author. | Staniford, Linda. From farm
to fork.
Title: How do animals give us food? / by Linda Staniford.
Other titles: Heinemann read and learn.
Description: Chicago, Illinois : Heinemann, [2016] | Series:
Heinemann read
    and learn | Series: From farm to fork | Includes
bibliographical
    references and index.
Identifiers: LCCN 2015046054| ISBN 9781484633502 (library
binding) | ISBN
    9781484633540 (pbk.) | ISBN 9781484633588 (ebook (pdf))
Subjects: LCSH: Meat--Juvenile literature. | Beef cattle--
Juvenile
    literature. | Food--Juvenile literature.
Classification: LCC TX371 .S78 2016 | DDC 641.3/6--dc23

Acknowledgments
The author and publisher are grateful to the following for
permission to reproduce copyright material: Alamy: Wayne
HUTCHINSON, 15; iStockphoto: Christopher Futcher, 5,
emholk, Cover Left, gabrieldome, 22 Bottom; Shutterstock:
Andrey Armyagov, Cover Right, Bildagentur Zoonar GmbH,
22 Middle, Bryan Sikora, 9, clearviewstock, 4, Evgeny
Litvinov, 18, Foodio, 17, Gerard Koudenburg, 14, Goncharuk
Maksim, 6, hans engbers, Cover Back, 13, K2 PhotoStudio,
22 Top, Lisovskaya Natalia, 21, majeczka, 10, Niloo, 16, Rob
Bouwman, 7, Robert Pernell, 19, Sergey Ryzhov, 20, smereka,
8, Volodymyr Kobzarenko, 11, zlikovec, 12.

Every effort has been made to contact copyright holders
of material reproduced in this book. Any omissions will
be rectified in subsequent printings if notice is given to
the publisher.

All the Internet addresses (URLs) given in this book were valid
at the time of going to press. However, due to the dynamic
nature of the Internet, some addresses may have changed, or
sites may have changed or ceased to exist since publication.
While the author and publisher regret any inconvenience this
may cause readers, no responsibility for any such changes can
be accepted by either the author or the publisher.

Some words are shown in bold, **like this**. You can find out
what they mean by looking in the glossary.

Table of Contents

Where Does Meat Come From?

Meat comes from animals. We get meat from a lot of different animals. Meat can come from cows, sheep, and chickens.

Meat contains **protein**. Protein is an important part of our diet. Our bodies need protein to stay healthy and strong.

What Other Food Do We Get from Animals?

We also get **dairy** foods from animals. Dairy foods include milk, cheese, and butter. Dairy foods also give us **protein**.

Another kind of animal that gives us food is fish. In this book we will look at how we get meat from cows.

Where Do Cows Live?

Cows live on farms. They eat grass
in fields. This is called grazing.

The farmer also feeds the cows hay in the winter. The farmer takes care of the cows. He makes sure they stay healthy.

How Big Are Farms?

Some farms are large. They have big fields with many animals. They may have other kinds of animals as well as cows.

Other farms are small. They have a few animals in a small field. The farmer gets **dairy** foods from his animals as well as meat.

Where Do Cows Come From?

A baby cow is called a calf. Calves (more than one calf) are born on farms. Their mothers feed the calves milk.

When they are older, the calves start to eat grass like their mothers. The calves grow big and strong.

What Happens When the Calves Are Older?

When the calves are big enough, the farmer takes them to an event called an auction. Here, people buy and sell animals such as calves.

At the auction, some of the calves are sold to other farmers. Other calves are sold to **butchers** for meat.

What Kind of Meat Do We Get from Cows?

Meat from cows is called beef. **Butchers** cut the beef into steaks, ribs, and more.

Beef can be also be **ground**. Ground beef can be made into hamburgers.

What Happens to the Beef?

Butchers store the beef in large
refrigerators. This keeps the beef fresh.
All kinds of meat can also be frozen
in freezers.

The beef is then packed into refrigerated trucks. The trucks take the beef to supermarkets and other stores. Beef is also sold in butchers' shops.

How Does Beef Get to Our Table?

Workers put the beef into **refrigerators** in stores. They group the same cuts of meat together.

We can choose the kind of beef we like to eat. The beef has come a long way from farm to fork!

All Kinds of Food from Animals!

Different animal meats that we eat include beef, chicken, turkey, and lamb.

Eggs are a good source of **protein**. Eggs come from chickens.

Salmon, trout, and cod are all popular fish that we eat.

Glossary

butcher person who cuts up and sells meat

dairy relating to milk and the products made from it, such as butter and cheese

ground cut or chopped into very small pieces

protein substance found in meat, cheese, eggs, and fish; our bodies need protein to stay healthy

refrigerator appliance for keeping our food cool

Find Out More

Books

Dickmann, Nancy. *Food from Farms* (World of Farming). Chicago: Heinemann Library, 2011.

Parker, Victoria. *All About Meat and Fish* (Food Zone). Irvine, Calif.: QEB, 2009.

Internet sites

Facthound offers a safe, fun way to find Internet sites related to this book. All of the sites on Facthound have been researched by our staff.

Here's all you do:
Visit www.facthound.com
Type in this code: 9781484633502

Index